A Writer's Journal

Lynée Gaillet
Georgia State University

Boston   Burr Ridge, IL   Dubuque, IA   Madison, WI   New York
San Francisco   St. Louis   Bangkok   Bogotá   Caracas   Kuala Lumpur
Lisbon   London   Madrid   Mexico City   Milan   Montreal   New Delhi
Santiago   Seoul   Singapore   Sydney   Taipei   Toronto

The McGraw·Hill Companies

 # Higher Education

Published by McGraw-Hill, an imprint of The McGraw-Hill Companies, Inc.,
1221 Avenue of the Americas, New York, NY 10020. Copyright © 2007. All
rights reserved. No part of this publication may be reproduced or distributed in
any form or by any means, or stored in a database or retrieval system, without
the prior written consent of The McGraw-Hill Companies, Inc., including, but
not limited to, in any network or other electronic storage or transmission, or
broadcast for distance learning.

This book is printed on acid-free paper.

1 2 3 4 5 6 7 8 9 0 DOC/DOC 0 9 8 7 6

ISBN-13: 978-0-07-326031-0
ISBN-10:   0-07-326031-2

Editor in Chief: *Emily Barrosse*
Publisher: *Lisa Moore*
Sponsoring Editor: *Christopher Bennem*
Marketing Manager: *Lori DeShazo*
Developmental Editor: *Betty Chen*
Production Editor: *Chanda Feldman*
Manuscript Editor: *Jan Fehler*
Design Manager: *Cassandra Chu*
Text and Cover Designer: *Maureen McCutcheon*
Art Editor: *Ayelet Arbel*
Production Supervisor: *Randy Hurst*
Composition: *11/13 New Century Schoolbook by TBH Typecast, Inc.*
Printing: *PMS 344, 45# New Era Matte, R. R. Donnelley & Sons*
Cover: Credit: © H. Wiesenhofer/PhotoLink / Getty Images

Library of Congress Control Number: 2006064421

The Internet addresses listed in the text were accurate at the time of publication. The inclusion of a Web site does not indicate an endorsement by the
authors or McGraw-Hill, and McGraw-Hill does not guarantee the accuracy of
the information presented at these sites.

www.mhhe.com

Contents

Acknowledgments

I wish to thank the following people for help with this project:

My Fall 2005 publication class for providing examples of the prewriting strategies, particularly Gina Henderson, Fran Holt-Underwood, Tish Nwoye, Xiumei Pu, Stacey Singer, Lara Smith, and Chris Stotelmyer.

Amanda Alligood, Ellen Alligood, Aaron Godbey, Samantha Johnson, Jamie Knack, Ashley Martin, and Elisabeth Sherwin for sharing their journal entries.

Lindsey Ryan Nelms, contributing editor, for her help formulating organizational patterns, soliciting samples, and editing prose.

Elizabeth Tasker, technical editor, for editing and preparing camera-ready copy.

Introduction

Collecting for Composing

You may have been asked to keep a journal for one of your classes before and, like many students, may have thought of the assignment as busy work. When journal keeping is imposed without a specific goal or purpose, the task easily becomes mundane or tedious. However, when you begin to consider yourself as a writer, your journal takes on new proportions and becomes a source for gleaning writing ideas and a place for growing your own compositions.

Many famous writers keep journals, commonplace books, or daybooks in which they collect their thoughts, possible topics for papers, rough drafts of ideas, observations of everyday life, and their responses to readings. By making regular entries in your journal, hopefully you will begin to think of yourself as a writer and not only as a student fulfilling a journal-keeping class requirement. By engaging in prewriting strategies and journal keeping, you may find increased significance in your responses to everyday events.

Writing is not a mysterious talent, but rather a skill to be learned—like driving a car or playing a musical instrument. Journal keeping will help you hone your writing abilities and perhaps make writing a less intimidating and more manageable process.

Why Keep a Journal?

Journal keeping is a personal record of your thoughts and opinions. This record is meant to be messy, disorganized, and generative—a place to try out new ideas that you might wish to explore further in formal writing assignments. Don't worry about editing your thoughts or following writing rules and conventions in your journal entries. Instead, try to get your ideas down on paper, express yourself without constraints or the worry that someone is looking over your shoulder or grading your early attempts. Be creative and inventive, explore issues that are new to you, try out writing styles that may feel foreign to you, without any risk.

Journal writing helps alleviate writer's block and is designed to help authors find a topic and something to say. The only way to improve as a writer is to practice writing. Your journal provides a safe place to try out new ideas and make mistakes as you begin to find your own voice and writing style.

How Do I Use This Journal?

Writing in class or only when your teacher requires you to compose for a grade will not provide enough practice to improve your writing skills. If you play a sport or an instrument, you already know that regular, scheduled practice is necessary to improve your game or performance. The same is true for writing.

Professional writers write every day—even when they aren't in the mood or think they don't have anything to say. Keep your journal notebook with you and record your thoughts as they occur or when you find yourself bored or with a few extra minutes on your hands—waiting in line or for appointments, or between classes. Find a regular time each day to record your thoughts; early in the morning or before bedtime works well for many writers. Use time in the morning to speculate about your day, or at night to reflect on the day's events.

The last sections of this book provide prompts, student samples, and plenty of space for you to try your hand at journal writing. You may write about whatever topics come to mind. The prompts and examples are designed to help you get started, not to confine your imagination or limit your possibilities. This part of the journal is divided into three sections: My Experiences (past), My World (present), and My Voice (future).

Prewriting Strategies

How do you begin writing? Come up with topics? Find evidence and support for your ideas? Organize your thoughts into coherent prose? Many writers brainstorm about their topics while going about everyday activities—shopping, driving, showering—but sometimes writer's block prohibits us from beginning writing projects.

Invention or heuristic prewriting strategies can help authors combat writer's block. These tested exercises offer tools for moving your writing forward and taking the mystery out of the writing process:

- Five Senses Chart
- Brainstorming and Listing
- Clustering
- Mapping
- Journalist's Questions
- Freewriting and Looping
- Interviewing
- Observation and Ethnographic Descriptions

The following sections offer a definition and sample for each prewriting strategy. On the blank pages provided, try your hand at each of these invention tools; discover which strategies work best for your specific assignment and personal work habits.

Five Senses Chart

This prewriting strategy asks you to evoke sensory images and sensations associated with an image, place, or object. By engaging in free association, you can generate a descriptive and creative list of details that will appeal to your readers' five senses—sight, sound, taste, smell, and touch.

Select a topic, then divide your page into five rows. List sensory details associated with your topic under the appropriate headings. Don't worry about filling in the chart systematically; just list impressions as they occur to you.

Five Senses Examples

	Mango
Sight	The outside is green with yellow spots and looks like a shell. The inside is a pale orange. The fruit looks stringy.—Some of it sticks to the shell as I peel it away, as it doesn't want to part from its protector.
Sound	Nothing, except when I eat it. I like to such on each piece I put in my mouth, so I can hear the swoosh of saliva and mango moving around.
Smell	Light and fresh. It promises a sweetness, which has a hint of ginger.
Taste	It is sweet but it has a spicy quality, a spark right at the end. It reminds me of ginger and cinnamon combined with a juicy wetness and a clean finish.
Touch	The outside: It's hard, hiding the soft innards. Also it's slippery smooth. When you hold it in your hand, it has the weight and feels solid. The Inside: It's squishy/sticky, and the juice gets all over your fingers, your face. The fruit is soft, malleable.—It's amazing how light it is when you peel it away from the seed in its center.

Try It: Five Senses Chart

	Subject/Topic:
Sight	
Sound	
Smell	
Taste	
Touch	

Try It: Five Senses Chart

	Subject/Topic:
Sight	
Sound	
Smell	
Taste	
Touch	

Try It: Five Senses Chart

Subject/Topic:
Sight
Sound
Smell
Taste
Touch

Try It: Five Senses Chart

	Subject/Topic:
Sight	
Sound	
Smell	
Taste	
Touch	

Try It: Five Senses Chart

	Subject/Topic:
Sight	
Sound	
Smell	
Taste	
Touch	

Brainstorming and Listing

This strategy involves jotting down all ideas related to a given topic. Abandon preconceived notions and predictable solutions in order to make room for innovative supporting ideas. Head your paper with a general topic, and then list whatever thoughts you have on the topic. By engaging in free association, you should produce a long list of ideas and supporting statements related to your topic. If you can't think of many items to list under the topic, then you might want to rethink your original idea.

Don't worry if you create many more ideas than you can accommodate on one paper. After compiling your list, go back and circle related ideas or the ones you think are best given the topic or length of your writing assignment.

Listing Example

TOPIC: *Does Technology Aid or Distract?*

Aids	Distractions
• Online databases	• Cell phones make driving dangerous
• Search engines	• Interrupts concentration
• Library catalog	• Inhibits creativity
• Conveying emergency information	• Encourages plagiarism
• Keeping in touch	• Exposes children to strangers
• Yellow pages	• False sense of security
• Mapquest	• Allows for less personal interaction
• Movie showtimes	• Less aware of surroundings
• Graphics	• Easy to lose cell phones, pagers, pdas
• Current news	• Expensive
• Emergency help	• Easy to play games instead of work
• Improves productivity	• No down time; always plugged in
• Ready reference	• Lost data if system crashes
• Grammar/spell checkers	

Try It: Listing

TOPIC: _____

_____

_____

_____

_____

_____

_____

_____

_____

_____

_____

_____

_____

_____

_____

_____

_____

_____

_____

_____

_____

_____

_____

_____

_____

_____

_____

_____

_____

Try It: Listing

TOPIC: _____

_____

_____

_____

_____

_____

_____

_____

_____

_____

_____

_____

_____

_____

_____

_____

_____

_____

_____

_____

_____

_____

_____

_____

_____

_____

_____

Try It: Listing

TOPIC: _____

_____

_____

_____

_____

_____

_____

_____

_____

_____

_____

_____

_____

_____

_____

_____

_____

_____

_____

_____

_____

_____

_____

_____

_____

_____

_____

_____

_____

Try It: Listing

TOPIC: _____

_____

_____

_____

_____

_____

_____

_____

_____

_____

_____

_____

_____

_____

_____

_____

_____

_____

_____

_____

_____

_____

_____

_____

_____

_____

_____

Try It: Listing

TOPIC: _____

_____

_____

_____

_____

_____

_____

_____

_____

_____

_____

_____

_____

_____

_____

_____

_____

_____

_____

_____

_____

_____

_____

_____

_____

_____

_____

_____

Clustering

Clustering is a visual prewriting strategy in which you map your ideas. This strategy is useful for sorting relationships between your thoughts and determining the main points you might wish to address in your paper. Clustering also helps you discover support for your primary ideas.

Start by writing your topic in the middle of the page. Then circle that main idea and draw connecting lines to related ideas. Continue this process until you have what might resemble a web, a flow chart, or wheel spokes on the page.

See the sample on the next page for clarification.

Clustering Example

TOPIC: *Why do students drop out of college?*

Try It: Clustering

TOPIC: _____

Try It: Clustering

TOPIC: _____

Try It: Clustering

TOPIC: _____

Try It: Clustering

TOPIC: _____

Try It: Clustering

TOPIC: _____

Mapping

Mapping is another visual prewriting strategy. By drawing a map, sketch, or floor plan, you make visual your abstract ideas. Mapping strategies sometimes include charts, graphs, street grids, or cartoons as well.

Use mapping techniques to literally think on paper. Your drawings, sketches, and doodles can help you generate ideas and supporting details. Don't worry if you're not artistic; stick figures and crude drawings serve the same purposes as detailed sketches for this exercise.

TOPIC: *My Family Farm*

Try It: Mapping

TOPIC: _____

Try It: Mapping

TOPIC: _____

Try It: Mapping

TOPIC: _____

Try It: Mapping

TOPIC: _____

Try It: Mapping

TOPIC: _____

Journalist's Questions

Adopting the questions asked by all good reporters (Who? What? Where? When? Why? and How?) will help you focus quickly on your topic and serve as an effective invention strategy. List each of these questions on a piece of paper, then list responses or answers to each query.

This strategy will help you establish patterns and related areas of interest, leading to subtopics and clear paragraph development. Don't worry about using all the information you generate. Pick and choose the ideas that seem best suited to your topic. This prewriting strategy is ideally suited for research papers.

Journalist's Questions Example

TOPIC: *Drilling in Alaska's Wildlife Refuge*

Who?	What?
United States and Congress (pass budget)	A bill was passed that opens Alaska's Wildlife Refuge to be drilled for oil.
Where?	**When?**
The bill was passed in Washington DC; but it will affect the environment/ population of Alaska.	On March 16, 2005, a Wednesday, a bill was passed in the Senate to open up the Refuge. Congress needs to pass a budget for the drilling before it begins.
Why?	**How?**
In order to fight rising oil prices and the looming energy crisis.	The Republicans put it on a bill that does not allow filibusters (an attempt to stop a decision from being taken by giving a long speech, which takes up the time available to vote/discuss alternate views), which is how the Democrats had kept the bill from being passed before.

Try It: Journalist's Questions

TOPIC:

Who?		What?	

Where?		When?	

Why?		How?	

Try It: Journalist's Questions

TOPIC:

Who?	What?

Where?	When?

Why?	How?

Try It: Journalist's Questions

TOPIC:

Who?

What?

Where?

When?

Why?

How?

Try It: Journalist's Questions

TOPIC:

Who?
_____
_____
_____
_____
_____
_____
_____
_____

What?
_____
_____
_____
_____
_____
_____
_____
_____

Where?
_____
_____
_____
_____
_____
_____
_____
_____

When?
_____
_____
_____
_____
_____
_____
_____
_____

Why?
_____
_____
_____
_____
_____
_____
_____
_____

How?
_____
_____
_____
_____
_____
_____
_____
_____

Try It: Journalist's Questions

TOPIC:

Who? _____
_____
_____
_____
_____
_____
_____
_____
_____

What? _____
_____
_____
_____
_____
_____
_____
_____
_____

Where? _____
_____
_____
_____
_____
_____
_____
_____
_____

When? _____
_____
_____
_____
_____
_____
_____
_____
_____

Why? _____
_____
_____
_____
_____
_____
_____
_____
_____

How? _____
_____
_____
_____
_____
_____
_____
_____
_____

Freewriting and Looping

Freewriting

This common prewriting strategy helps authors generate a writing topic and supporting details. For many writers, freewriting helps stave off writer's block by providing a risk-free opportunity for finding a topic. While freewriting, you should write about anything that comes to mind for a pre-scribed time, usually ten or fifteen minutes. Don't stop writing until time is up. If you get stuck, write about your day thus far or even your frustrations with the activity. For many writers, just getting words out of the head and onto paper leads to possible topics for writing.

When freewriting, don't stop to edit your work or revise your ideas. The goal is to produce a block of prose that will yield the germ of an idea that you can then explore and expand into a more developed piece.

Looping

Looping is an extension of freewriting. Once you have pro-duced an initial freewriting sample, go back and circle your best ideas, words, and phrases from that piece. Repeat the freewriting exercise (writing for a specified time without stop-ping) on one of the circled topics or phrases. Repeat the freewriting and looping exercise two or three times; each attempt should help focus your writing a bit more. By the end of the exercise, you may have a thesis and supporting details for an extended piece of writing.

Freewriting and Looping Samples

FREEWRITING TOPIC: *Rebellion*

Today I was thinking about rebellion. It comes from my class because the teacher said we are all rebels but I don't think half of the kids in here have ever rebelled about anything in their lives and it is so hard to do this. I guess this is rebelling because I don't want to do it and I don't understand how writing without thinking about it helps me do anything at all except wear out my fingers and they really hurt and I can't think about what I'm writing because my fingers hurt and now I've misspelled things and she said not go back and fix them and I really want everything I write to be perfect and it is not and I can't make it work but that's not really rebellion I'm just tired and to write for ten minutes seems to be impossible and my clock on the computer says it has only been four minutes and I have five more to go so what can I say about rebellion? What about in high school and all of the students were told that they couldn't have "unnatural" hair colors so they bought wigs and my mom came down to the school and tried to talk to the principle and Mr. Wolff just wouldn't listen and we all camped out on the front steps until our parents were called. My mom didn't care of course, she went with me to have my eyebrow pierced and helped me do my hair half of the time. That is sort of rebellion but it didn't work because we still couldn't have purple or green hair and someone got suspended the next week for having a nose ring but we felt like we made it at graduation because my whole group of friends tucked red and blue hair (our school colors) up under our mortarboards until the end when we flung them in the air and poor Mr. Wolff had a heart attack two weeks after and almost died and Mrs. Whatshername got the job. Lots of the other kids had other neat ways of rebelling but we just wanted to have a good time and be "individuals". So I think my friends and our hair and our piercings are the best topic and thank god the buzzer just rang.

Looping:

In high school, my friends and I were obsessed with maintaining a sense of "individuality". We did everything we could to stand out, even when it meant breaking the rules of our strict private high school. We dyed our hair every color of the rainbow and got as many piercings as we were allowed. My parents always taught me to be myself. They didn't necessarily approve of what I did to my appearance but if I made a good enough argument, I could get away with a lot more than most kids. My mom even signed the papers (that so many kids had to fake) that gave me permission to get my eyebrow pierced! I walked around feeling cooler than anyone else, even when our administrators made me put a bandage over my piercing. Since I graduated and have started college, I've started to realize that what really makes people stand out is not hair or style but attitude and intelligence. Plus, I think it's funny that for all of our efforts to be different, my friends and I ended up looking like clones of one another.

Try It: Freewriting and Looping

TOPIC: _____

_____

_____

_____

_____

_____

_____

_____

_____

_____

_____

_____

_____

_____

_____

_____

_____

_____

_____

_____

_____

_____

_____

_____

_____

_____

_____

Try It: Freewriting and Looping

TOPIC: _____

_____

_____

_____

_____

_____

_____

_____

_____

_____

_____

_____

_____

_____

_____

_____

_____

_____

_____

_____

_____

_____

_____

_____

_____

_____

_____

_____

_____

Try It: Freewriting and Looping

TOPIC: _____

Try It: Freewriting and Looping

TOPIC: _____

_____

_____

_____

_____

_____

_____

_____

_____

_____

_____

_____

_____

_____

_____

_____

_____

_____

_____

_____

_____

_____

_____

_____

_____

_____

Try It: Freewriting and Looping

TOPIC: _____

_____

_____

_____

_____

_____

_____

_____

_____

_____

_____

_____

_____

_____

_____

_____

_____

_____

_____

_____

_____

_____

_____

_____

_____

_____

_____

_____

_____

Interviewing

Sometimes asking questions of your topic, or an imagined (or even real) person involved in the subject you are researching, can help jumpstart your project. You may conduct this interview either aloud or on paper. After selecting a general topic, try dividing your paper into two columns, one for listing questions and one for answers.

This prewriting tool is helpful for exploring two sides of an issue, developing a refutation section for a persuasive paper, or gathering evidence in support of a position.

Interviewing Example

TOPIC: *Interview Questions and Answers for an Actor*

	Questions	Answers
1.	What is your name—do you use a real name or a stage name?	Dan Drama. This is a stage name. My real name is Daniel Dramaniski. That just seemed too long for people to remember and pronounce.
2.	When did you realize that you wanted to become an actor?	When I was in sixth grade. My mom encouraged me to try out for the school musical. I got a good part and loved being on stage. From then on I looked for opportunities to act.
3.	What was your first performance?	As the lion in the <u>Wizard of Oz</u> in the sixth grade.
4.	What was your favorite performance and why?	My favorite performance was as Willy Loman in Arthur Miller's <u>Death of a Salesman.</u> I performed this at the Ashland, Oregon Shakespeare Festival in the summer of 1995. I love the passion of that role and the challenge of playing someone so serious and disturbed.

Questions	Answers
5. Where and from whom did you learn the most to prepare for an acting career?	While working in New York waiting tables and trying out for bit parts. I was in a community of actors, who through daily conversations, taught me about the ins and outs of auditions and acting. You learned by doing it, being there, wanting it.
6. What actors do you look to as role models and why?	The ones I appreciate most are actors like William H. Macy and Philip Hoffman Seymour, who are character actors, working because they love to act and have a way of transforming themselves into so many roles without standing out as a movie icon. They do tv, stage, and film; they are full range.
7. Who was instrumental in helping you become an actor?	My parents and my high school drama teacher. They helped me map out a plan and encouraged me along the way.
8. How do you prepare for a role?	First, I really learn the script. Then, link the character to things in my experience and life. I also try to talk to the writer and spend time with real people who match those roles. For example, as a doctor, I might hang out at a hospital and just watch doctors talk and move.
9. Do you prefer stage, tv or film work?	Live stage work is my favorite. All the elements come together and you have immediate audience reaction. It is very powerful.
10. What is your favorite movie?	Hard to say. As a child, The Cowboys. Maybe The Usual Suspects for acting and script writing. Then, I also love creative ones like Momento or Magnolia.

Try It: Interviewing

TOPIC: _____	
Questions	*Answers*

Try It: Interviewing

TOPIC: _____

Questions	Answers

Try It: Interviewing

TOPIC:	
Questions	*Answers*

Try It: Interviewing

TOPIC: _____

Questions	Answers

Try It: Interviewing

TOPIC: _____

Questions	Answers

Observation and Ethnographic Descriptions

Direct observation is one of the best strategies for generating paper ideas and details. Visit places you want to write about and closely observe public spaces, participants' behavior, or objects. Recording your observations will give you concrete sensory details and facts to support your thesis. This strategy is particularly useful for writing papers in the social sciences.

Visit your "site" with notebook and pencil in hand, paying particular attention to sensory details (the sound of a waterfall or kids' laughter at a park), physical layout (traffic patterns at the mall), and personal relationships (Saturday night courtship rituals at the movies). In your paper, reflect on your observations. What do you make of the events you've witnessed? Rather than answering the journalist questions of who? what? where? when? why? and how?, ethnographers examine relationships among participants and their environments, making observations about behavior, group dynamics, or cultural backgrounds. Your notes and descriptions provide the evidence to support assumptions you make about cultural groups or artifacts.

Observation Example

TOPIC: *Describe an artifact from local museum*

Courtesy of the Michael C. Carlos Museum of Emory University. Photo by Bruce White.

This marble relief is the grave <u>stele</u> of an unknown man from Greece and is dated ca. 400 B.C. The description accompanying the relief provided the terminology and basic historical information that, combined with my own observations, constitutes the following analysis.

The scene depicted here is of a banquet. The man reclines on a <u>kline</u> (couch) opposite his wife and holds a small <u>phiale</u> (dish). A serving boy stands before a large volute krater and holds both the man's <u>rhyton</u> (drinking horn) and an <u>oinochoe</u> (small pitcher). In the background is a prominent horse's head, a common motif of the period indicating status. From this description, and the solid crafts-manship of the relief, it is safe to assume that this man was probably wealthy and enjoyed some prominence in society.

This relief adheres to the traditional profile view with the torsos slightly angled toward the viewer. In each case two individuals face one another and are gesturing with their hands: the figure on the left is giving or preparing something and the figure on the right is accepting. The scene is somewhat formal and gives the impression that the individuals actually posed for the artist, although this is unlikely.

The relief is about three feet long and perhaps two feet tall. Originally the scene would have been framed by architectural elements and the name of the deceased inscribed above the scene. The work is displayed against a wall with lights illuminating it from above and sits on a "shelf" about five feet high, bringing it to the average eye-level. The accompanying description is thorough and informative and sets the object in the proper historical context regarding its influences and motifs. The Greek word for each object is provided and a brief explanation of the "banquet scene" motif is provided.

Seeing a 2,400 year-old marble relief brought from the other side of the world and displayed inches away from me was a humbling experience. Had I been permitted I would have touched it to get a sense of its texture and depth. Who, in ancient times, would ever have guessed that a modest grave marker of now unknown man would be such a marvel?

Ethnography Example

TOPIC: *Describe what you observe at a public place.*

Last Chance Thrift Store:

Standing in the checkout lane, I had a perfect view to the back of the store where the lamps sat for sale on a top shelf. The lampshades were missing, so they sat like plump old women, dolled up and missing a vital part to complete their outfit. The store had fluorescent lights and long, squat rows of used clothes. With the large number of customers, it was stifling to walk among them, shifting through ratty, stained clothes for that one priceless gem. There was a lot of "Excuse mes," and "I'm sorries, I didn't mean to bump yous." The clientele was a mix between stylish ladies, who didn't need to shop at a thrift store; they were just slumming a little; and young college students like me, who were caught between Macy's and second-hand stores: our only way to afford the first was to shop regularly at the latter. Then there were the women, with a kid in the cart and one hiding under the clothes rake, who were buying the kids some new clothes. And as I looked at the child sitting cross-legged on the floor, I thought about the ingrained dirt and the grime. I hadn't even taken off my shoes, when I tried on some pants in the changing room, and here this little boy was patting the floor.

As I finalized my purchase, I noted the wheel chairs and shopping carts haphazardly organized by the entrance to the store. Funny, I hadn't noticed them on the way in; they were almost blocking my exit now. I walked out and noticed the mildew growing out of the pavement, and the tarnished bench where an older man sat nonchalantly reading a newspaper. As I reached my car, I looked back at that dungeounous entrance: it looked liked a subway entrance, going down to caverns below. You couldn't even see the entrance doors from the street. All you could see were old pillars, once white, now cream and green from lack of care, rising up to the mauve awning, old and rusty. Up top was a metal design. It had an orange center, with yellow rays coming out. It belonged on a boardwalk with games, cotton candy, taffy, and the sound of oceans rolling into the beach; not here in a worn-out shopping plaza, long abandoned for new development, with cars parked and grime leaking out in all directions. Yet people came there to shop, and a man read a newspaper outside.

Try It: Observation/Ethnography

TOPIC: _____

_____
_____
_____
_____
_____
_____
_____
_____
_____
_____
_____
_____
_____
_____
_____
_____
_____
_____
_____
_____
_____
_____
_____
_____
_____
_____
_____
_____
_____

Try It: Observation/Ethnography

TOPIC: _____

_____

_____

_____

_____

_____

_____

_____

_____

_____

_____

_____

_____

_____

_____

_____

_____

_____

_____

_____

_____

_____

_____

_____

_____

_____

_____

_____

Try It: Observation/Ethnography

TOPIC: _____

_____

_____

_____

_____

_____

_____

_____

_____

_____

_____

_____

_____

_____

_____

_____

_____

_____

_____

_____

_____

_____

_____

_____

_____

_____

_____

_____

Try It: Observation/Ethnography

TOPIC: _____

_____

_____

_____

_____

_____

_____

_____

_____

_____

_____

_____

_____

_____

_____

_____

_____

_____

_____

_____

_____

_____

_____

_____

_____

_____

_____

_____

_____

Try It: Observation/Ethnography

TOPIC: _____

_____

_____

_____

_____

_____

_____

_____

_____

_____

_____

_____

_____

_____

_____

_____

_____

_____

_____

_____

_____

_____

_____

_____

_____

_____

_____

_____

_____

_____

_____

_____

_____

Occasions
for Writing

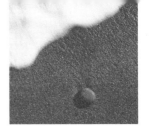

The Greek philosopher Aristotle defined three occasions or rhetorical settings for making speeches or arguments. Aristotle's divisions are now famous and correspond with three different locations in time: forensic writing and speeches are located in the past, epideictic rhetoric is located in the present; and deliberative writing and speeches look to the future.

Although Aristotle's rules of communication originally applied to speech making, many composition teachers and textbooks have borrowed his ideas and applied them to writing instruction. The next three sections of this journal, "My Experiences (Past/Forensic)," "My World (Present/Epideictic)," and "My Voice (Future/Deliberative)," define Aristotle's three occasions for writing and present sample student essays and lists of topics to help you get started keeping your own journal. The prompts and examples are meant to encourage a variety of responses. Use your imagination and the prewriting strategies we've discussed to generate unique topics for your papers and assignments.

My Experiences: Past/Forensic

When we write about the past, we try to gain perspective on events and experiences. For Aristotle, forensic rhetoric reconstructed the past in order to find evidence to support claims. In ancient Greece, forensic speeches addressed questions of justice and issues of right and wrong. The forensic speaker asked listeners to examine their beliefs about justice and values concerning society.

For us, writing about the past helps us understand both ourselves and different cultures a little better. By reading personal stories, as readers, we too examine our belief systems and test out our values against varying societal norms.

This section provides three writing prompts and samples of student writing addressing the following topics:

- *What physical feature would you change about yourself?*
- *Who is your family?*
- *What assumption did you have as a child that you have found to be incorrect?*

The student samples are varied and hopefully will show you there is no right way to address the writing prompts. At the end of this section are additional ideas or heuristic strategies to help you get started writing about the past.

Sample Student Journal Exercise

TOPIC: *What physical feature would you change about yourself?*

 I remember that I used to feel very unhappy with my square-shaped face. I was born and raised in China, so I always wished I could have an oval-shaped one, the ideal face shape for a Chinese beauty. I had heard and read that every woman of legendary Chinese beauty had oval-shaped faces. Being born with a square face, which is conventionally better suited for a boy rather than a girl, annoys me.

 However, I have gradually grown to accept my face. First of all, Chinese astrology says that a person with a square face has the potential for intelligence, fortitude, and a promising career. Since girls of my generation are expected to have a career and take care of ourselves, I feel happy that I am pulled in that direction with my square face. More importantly, I have discovered that the criteria for beauty can be very different across cultural borders. I was astonished to see one of my American girl classmates wearing an artificial red flower in her hair, believing she was beautiful. An artificial red flower worn in the hair in China is an indication of prostitution. I was equally shocked when my American host pointed at a picture she took in Tibet and commented that the middle-aged woman in the picture with exposed gums looked "amazingly beautiful" because in Chinese culture a person who exposes their gums is considered ugly and doomed to die young. The list of differences between American and Chinese perceptions of beauty can extend as long as the Great Wall.

 Although I never heard anyone tell me I am a beautiful girl in China, I impress more and more of my American classmates and friends as good-looking. I understand that they judge my appearance from a perspective very different or even oppositional to Chinese criteria. Beautiful or not is only a matter of social encoding. Upon discovering that the concept of beauty is arbitrary, fluid, and ambiguous, I have stopped being annoyed by my physical feature.

Xiumei Pu

Sample Student Journal Exercise

TOPIC: *What physical feature would you change about yourself?*

One physical feature I would change about myself would be my height and size. I would want to be shorter, and not too skinny. I do not like being so skinny because it makes me look even taller than I am. Also, being so tall makes me look skinnier.

One of the reasons I don't like being tall is because I can't where cute shoes. Whenever I see a pair of shoes I like, they are always high heels. I used to where high heels, but I don't anymore. They make me look so tall that I tower over people. Whenever I do where high heels, or even boots with thick soles, people make comments about how tall I am. I don't like being so tall because it makes me stick out.

Being skinny, I feel like I have no figure or shape. It's hard for me to find pants that fit me right. The pants have to be small so they can fit around my waist, but yet they have to be big so they will be long enough. I could get pants in a small size, and a longer length, but the only stores that carry long lengths are expensive stores that I can't afford. My mom says I'm crazy to want to change the way I look. When I tell other people that I don't like being tall or skinny they sometimes tell me that wished they looked like me. I guess they will never know what it's like until they are actually in my shoes.

Ashley Martin

Sample Student Journal Exercise

TOPIC: *Who is your family?*

My parents bought a farm, and then they bought another farm-like property. Their empty-nest needed to be filled, and what's better to fill up a nest then birds? So they bought farms and then chickens and turkeys and pheasants and peacocks. Now Big Gene and Sharon have a smorgasbord of feathered friends.

My parents have birds, and I write chickens and peacocks into my poetry to talk about my family. Also, when I'm not writing about them (both parents and turkeys), I feed them when I go home for a visit. I don't know why I'm writing about it now, but there's something so comforting, so "my family" in these birds and farms.

My parents are both dentists, crazy kids that just constantly have a ball. I mean, my mom graduated from dental school with two other woman— the largest number her school ever graduated at that point. She had people walk out on her when she first started practicing; for some people, there was no way a <u>woman</u> was doing a filling on them. I never knew that though, because she only told me recently, sitting out at the farm. It's just that my mom was always doing what made her happy and so did my father, even when others didn't approve.

They've taught me that hard work combined with silliness is what life is all about. When they retire, they want to take the farms on fulltime; Mom in her garden, Dad on the tractor. So many of their friends think they're crazy, but they're just having a good time. I hope that when I get older I can find some new adventure to go on like them.

Gina Henderson

Sample Student Journal Exercise

TOPIC: *Who is your family?*

I realized that the folks that I consider family are not all related to me by blood. My mother, father, sister, grandmothers, grandfathers, aunts, uncles, cousins, and even family cat were all part of my family growing up, but some of the people I love the most are not actually related to me. I got this great gift when I was born, my mother asked her friend, Cookie, and Cookie's husband, Tom, to be my godparents. I call them "Aunt O" and "Uncle Tom." They, along with their two sons, are more present in my life than any other family members. I grew up seeing them, talking to them, and learning from them. The boys are like brothers to me.

This family was so present in my days, my weeks, my thoughts, and my prayers. Aunt O and Uncle Tom remembered my birthdays with phone calls, cards, and special gifts. Uncle Tom gave me my first pearl earrings. Aunt O taught me about faith and caring. She gave me her favorite bracelet when she was a child. Her wedding dress was given to me. Summer vacations included visits to their house. They would plan days in San Francisco, weekends to horse shows, or just dinners at home. I had long talks with my godmother about being a woman and what I wanted to do with my life. My godfather would call me to get college basketball game scores when he was traveling for work and offered pieces of advice about boys, careers, and always encouraged me along life's path. They planted seeds and nurtured them, as I grew older. When I moved away, they came to visit me.

As time went on, I lost "true" family members and it was my godmother who could comfort me when my mother and father were no longer present. She makes needlepoint Christmas ornaments and sends emails telling me she loves me and believes in me. When my godfather died, I participated in the memorial service with his two sons. I was like his daughter. I am his daughter in many ways. In preparing the eulogy, I realized how much he loved me and cared for me even though I wasn't even his true relative.

Family definitely includes those we are related to, but it also includes those who just love us and give us time, encouragement and a place in their lives. Sometimes the greatest gifts we get from our blood relatives are relationships with those people that are special to them.

Lara Smith

Sample Student Journal Exercise

TOPIC: *What assumption did you have as a child that you have found to be incorrect?*

I assumed my parents would always be together, and that their marriage and our family would always be perfect. As a young child, I placed my parents on a pedestal. They were perfect, and they were mine. The naive innocence of a child told me life was great. Nothing was too big for my parents to repair. My child-sized faith led me to believe in an eternally pleasant world.

All too soon, I realized this assumption was false. My father made poor life choices that tore our family apart, and there was nothing any of us could do. My parents separated and then divorced a few years later. It turns out to be a positive change, but my views and assumptions about marriage and family life are changed forever. Marriage is a big commitment. Now, more than ever, I realize this fact. It is not something to be taken lightly. Before I marry, I am going to make sure I know my future husband extremely well. It is important that we both understand the magnitude of the commitment we are making. Marriage should be for life.

Love is an emotion; commitment is a choice. I choose to accept reality as it is and commit to a lifelong marriage of trust, respect, and love. Assumptions based on childhood innocence are great, but life moves on, and so I learn from my past idealism along the way.

Ellen Alligood

Sample Student Journal Exercise

TOPIC: *What assumption did you have as a child that you have found to be incorrect?*

Growing up in Catholic school caused me to have a sheltered view of what the real world was like. I mean, I remember when I was 13 or 14 I was amazed to discover that all people weren't Catholics. Silly, I know, but it shows how little of the world I had experienced.

Even though I've had many religious assumptions blown out of the water with age and maturity, I've become more fascinated with a bigger social assumption I've grown to be wary of. When I was younger, I was impressed by people who could be articulate and clever. I assumed that if a person could be amusing and entertaining than they must be a nice person. To me, joviality equaled a truly good-natured person.

Yet, as I grow older I find that just because someone can tell funny stories or jokes doesn't mean that they are necessarily a "good" person. Many people who can get you laughing so hard that your sides hurt can also be the people who might not pay you back that twenty bucks they owe you. Also, those same people that make interesting comments about the reality of the government, the world, science, etc. also might leave a friend stranded in the middle of nowhere.

I realize now that good people do not always have to be the cleverest folks, but they're continually genuine in word and deed. I find that people that speak from their hearts are the best kind of "good" person. They are also the most rare.

Gina Henderson

Other Writing Prompts about the Past

- What is the most difficult task you've ever accomplished?
- Given the events of the Terry Schiavo case, what are your thoughts about living wills?
- What is the most frightening experience from your childhood?
- How do you want people to remember you?
- Do you have faith in Homeland Security?
- If you could go back to any age, what would it be and why?
- Recalling your own experiences or observations, do you think parents should stay together for the sake of the children?

Journal Exercise

DATE: _____

TOPIC: _____

_____
_____
_____
_____
_____
_____
_____
_____
_____
_____
_____
_____
_____
_____
_____
_____
_____
_____
_____
_____
_____
_____
_____
_____
_____
_____
_____
_____

Journal Exercise

DATE: _____

TOPIC: _____

_____

_____

_____

_____

_____

_____

_____

_____

_____

_____

_____

_____

_____

_____

_____

_____

_____

_____

_____

_____

_____

_____

_____

Journal Exercise

DATE: _____

TOPIC: _____

_____
_____
_____
_____
_____
_____
_____
_____
_____
_____
_____
_____
_____
_____
_____
_____
_____
_____
_____
_____
_____
_____
_____
_____
_____
_____
_____
_____
_____

Journal Exercise

DATE: _____

TOPIC: _____

_____

_____

_____

_____

_____

_____

_____

_____

_____

_____

_____

_____

_____

_____

_____

_____

_____

_____

_____

_____

_____

_____

_____

_____

Journal Exercise

DATE: _____

TOPIC: _____

_____

_____

_____

_____

_____

_____

_____

_____

_____

_____

_____

_____

_____

_____

_____

_____

_____

_____

_____

_____

_____

_____

_____

_____

_____

_____

Journal Exercise

DATE: _____

TOPIC: _____

_____

_____

_____

_____

_____

_____

_____

_____

_____

_____

_____

_____

_____

_____

_____

_____

_____

_____

_____

_____

_____

_____

_____

_____

_____

_____

Journal Exercise

DATE: _____

TOPIC: _____

_____

_____

_____

_____

_____

_____

_____

_____

_____

_____

_____

_____

_____

_____

_____

_____

_____

_____

_____

_____

_____

_____

_____

_____

_____

_____

_____

_____

Journal Exercise

DATE: _____

TOPIC: _____

_____

_____

_____

_____

_____

_____

_____

_____

_____

_____

_____

_____

_____

_____

_____

_____

_____

_____

_____

_____

_____

_____

_____

_____

_____

Journal Exercise

DATE: _____

TOPIC: _____

_____
_____
_____
_____
_____
_____
_____
_____
_____
_____
_____
_____
_____
_____
_____
_____
_____
_____
_____
_____
_____
_____
_____
_____
_____
_____
_____
_____
_____

Journal Exercise

DATE: _____

TOPIC: _____

_____
_____
_____
_____
_____
_____
_____
_____
_____
_____
_____
_____
_____
_____
_____
_____
_____
_____
_____
_____
_____
_____
_____
_____
_____
_____

Journal Exercise

DATE: _____

TOPIC: _____

_____

_____

_____

_____

_____

_____

_____

_____

_____

_____

_____

_____

_____

_____

_____

_____

_____

_____

_____

_____

_____

_____

_____

_____

_____

_____

_____

_____

_____

Journal Exercise

DATE: _____

TOPIC: _____

_____
_____
_____
_____
_____
_____
_____
_____
_____
_____
_____
_____
_____
_____
_____
_____
_____
_____
_____
_____
_____
_____
_____

Journal Exercise

DATE: _____

TOPIC: _____

_____

_____

_____

_____

_____

_____

_____

_____

_____

_____

_____

_____

_____

_____

_____

_____

_____

_____

_____

_____

_____

_____

_____

_____

_____

_____

_____

_____

_____

_____

_____

Journal Exercise

DATE: _____

TOPIC: _____

_____

_____

_____

_____

_____

_____

_____

_____

_____

_____

_____

_____

_____

_____

_____

_____

_____

_____

_____

_____

_____

_____

_____

Journal Exercise

DATE: _____

TOPIC: _____

_____

_____

_____

_____

_____

_____

_____

_____

_____

_____

_____

_____

_____

_____

_____

_____

_____

_____

_____

_____

_____

_____

_____

_____

_____

_____

_____

_____

Journal Exercise

DATE: _____

TOPIC: _____

_____
_____
_____
_____
_____
_____
_____
_____
_____
_____
_____
_____
_____
_____
_____
_____
_____
_____
_____
_____
_____
_____
_____
_____
_____
_____
_____

Journal Exercise

DATE: _____

TOPIC: _____

_____

_____

_____

_____

_____

_____

_____

_____

_____

_____

_____

_____

_____

_____

_____

_____

_____

_____

_____

_____

_____

_____

_____

_____

_____

_____

Journal Exercise

DATE: _____

TOPIC: _____

_____

_____

_____

_____

_____

_____

_____

_____

_____

_____

_____

_____

_____

_____

_____

_____

_____

_____

_____

_____

_____

_____

_____

_____

Journal Exercise

DATE: _____

TOPIC: _____

_____
_____
_____
_____
_____
_____
_____
_____
_____
_____
_____
_____
_____
_____
_____
_____
_____
_____
_____
_____
_____
_____
_____
_____
_____
_____
_____
_____

Journal Exercise

DATE: _____

TOPIC: _____

_____

_____

_____

_____

_____

_____

_____

_____

_____

_____

_____

_____

_____

_____

_____

_____

_____

_____

_____

_____

_____

_____

_____

Journal Exercise

DATE: _____

TOPIC: _____

_____
_____
_____
_____
_____
_____
_____
_____
_____
_____
_____
_____
_____
_____
_____
_____
_____
_____
_____
_____
_____
_____
_____
_____
_____
_____

Journal Exercise

DATE: _____

TOPIC: _____

_____

_____

_____

_____

_____

_____

_____

_____

_____

_____

_____

_____

_____

_____

_____

_____

_____

_____

_____

_____

_____

_____

_____

_____

_____

_____

Journal Exercise

DATE: _____

TOPIC: _____

_____
_____
_____
_____
_____
_____
_____
_____
_____
_____
_____
_____
_____
_____
_____
_____
_____
_____
_____
_____
_____
_____
_____
_____
_____
_____
_____
_____

Journal Exercise

DATE: _____

TOPIC: _____

_____

_____

_____

_____

_____

_____

_____

_____

_____

_____

_____

_____

_____

_____

_____

_____

_____

_____

_____

_____

_____

_____

_____

_____

_____

Journal Exercise

DATE: _____

TOPIC: _____

_____
_____
_____
_____
_____
_____
_____
_____
_____
_____
_____
_____
_____
_____
_____
_____
_____
_____
_____
_____
_____
_____
_____
_____
_____
_____

Journal Exercise

DATE: _____

TOPIC: _____

_____

_____

_____

_____

_____

_____

_____

_____

_____

_____

_____

_____

_____

_____

_____

_____

_____

_____

_____

_____

_____

_____

_____

_____

Journal Exercise

DATE: _____

TOPIC: _____

_____
_____
_____
_____
_____
_____
_____
_____
_____
_____
_____
_____
_____
_____
_____
_____
_____
_____
_____
_____
_____
_____
_____
_____
_____
_____
_____
_____

Journal Exercise

DATE: _____

TOPIC: _____

_____

_____

_____

_____

_____

_____

_____

_____

_____

_____

_____

_____

_____

_____

_____

_____

_____

_____

_____

_____

_____

_____

_____

_____

_____

Journal Exercise

DATE: _____

TOPIC: _____

_____

_____

_____

_____

_____

_____

_____

_____

_____

_____

_____

_____

_____

_____

_____

_____

_____

_____

_____

_____

_____

_____

_____

_____

Journal Exercise

DATE: _____

TOPIC: _____

_____

_____

_____

_____

_____

_____

_____

_____

_____

_____

_____

_____

_____

_____

_____

_____

_____

_____

_____

_____

_____

_____

_____

_____

_____

_____

My World: Present/Epideictic

When we write about the present, we examine commonly held beliefs, current events, and our responses to the world. For Aristotle, epideictic rhetoric (set in the present) also concerned contemporary events, usually involving ceremonial speeches dealing with praise or blame. Examples of epideictic rhetoric from ancient Greece include funeral orations, praise for local heroes, or public condemnation of bad politicians. For Aristotle, epideictic speeches and writings reinforced commonly held beliefs and upheld values such as honesty, beauty, courage, and bravery.

For us, writing about the present helps us gain perspective on our changing world and perhaps question commonly held beliefs and values.

This section provides three writing prompts and samples of student writing addressing the following topics.

- *Does technology aid or distract?*
- *What does the concept of spirituality mean to you?*
- *Describe your personal rebellion.*

The student samples are varied and hopefully will show you a range of ways you might respond to these writing prompts. You can find additional ideas or heuristic strategies at the end of this section to help you get started writing about the present.

Sample Student Journal Exercise

TOPIC: *Does technology aid or distract?*

    While in the library this afternoon, I was forced to listen to several conversations conducted on cell phones. I find it strange that an individual would not feel self-conscious or embarrassed by talking on their cell phone in a library. Not even libraries are safe from cell phones anymore it seems. I enjoy quiet moments and particularly enjoy libraries, but I think that silence is becoming an antiquated idea.

    I notice that some people say things on their cell phone that strike me as private or even inappropriate for a public place. Last week I heard a woman ask her cell phone interlocutor "I have something to tell you but you have to keep it a secret." She then proceeded to tell her friend the secret. Furthermore, she was talking loudly and clearly, as many often do on cell phones. Fortunately, I wasn't the only one to notice the irony—several people nearby chuckled.

    People are beginning to lose awareness of their surroundings, which could be dangerous if you happen to be driving a car. I am not sure of the statistics but I would imagine that a certain percentage of auto accidents are caused by cell phone usage. If the percentage gets high enough, insurance companies may demand legislation to prohibit cell phone use while driving. Some states already have laws that require hands-free headsets for driving. I doubt that most consumers would push for this kind of legislation because so many people would never want to limit their cell phone use.

    Chris Stotelmyer

Sample Student Journal Exercise

TOPIC: *Does technology aid or distract?*

Most students can get distracted from studying by anything. I know that when I go to study everything looks more interesting than actually sitting down to study. I do not have ADD, but how would want to study for a class when you reading a favorite book or watching television? I think that TV and video games are definitely a distraction. The Internet, on the other hand, helps students to study.

The Internet now contains so much information that whatever you are looking for can be found with little struggle. This helps when a student is studying for a topic that they know nothing about. I do not think that any of these forms of technology creates or contributes to ADD. Both my brother and I were raised the same way and he has ADD and I do not. I think that if a person's activities consist only of TV watching and Internet surfing, they might gain weight, but they won't necessarily get ADD.

Samantha Johnson

Sample Student Journal Exercise

TOPIC: *What does the concept of spirituality mean to you?*

I've always found it interesting that all of the major religions espouse some version of the Golden Rule: "Do unto others as you would have them do unto you." If all of these religions agree on something so fundamental, why is there so much violence between religious groups? The problem, I think, lies not in the religions themselves, but in some of the human beings who claim to practice certain religions. I suspect that it is precisely because human beings have the capacity for such horrible violence that religion was conceived of in the first place. There is no doubt in my mind that religion has had a positive influence on history, and that without religion whole civilizations would not exist. Regardless, I often find it difficult to reconcile the positive influence of religion with the crimes committed in its name.

I think part of the problem is also that we value material objects so highly. This is true not only in America but in countries all over the world—our obsession with material things has made us selfish. The honest pursuit of religion is difficult; it requires one to give up part of the self in favor of others, and a society in which individuals are intent upon self-gratification and luxury can hardly be open to self-sacrifice. This need to accumulate extends from individuals to whole countries, particularly when land or other resources are at stake. I would guess that oil, for instance, has been the cause of as many or more deaths than some religions. No, religion is not the problem. Human beings—flawed and imperfect—are responsible for there own miseries. Likewise, human beings are responsible for relieving those miseries.

Chris Stotelmyer

Sample Student Journal Exercise

TOPIC: *What does the concept of spirituality mean to you?*

I met this woman recently whose spirituality was so present that it seemed to seep from her body and float in the air. It was a sunny Friday morning. I was rushed, anxious, and nervous on my way to see her. I was interviewing her for an article I was writing about abstract art shows. I did not know much about her other than that we had a mutual friend and that she had an exhibition opening soon.

On my way, I was cursing traffic and myself for being late. My cell phone rang and this sweet, soft voice said, "Lara, this is Rosa. Do you like eggs?" She had gone to the store to buy things for breakfast. Our meeting was early and she was concerned that I had not eaten. Her hospitality melted my edginess. She said she sensed that I stayed busy and might welcome a chance to sit and eat.

She greeted me outside of her studio apartment with a gentle hug and a warm, rich smile. As she cooked eggs, heated croissants, and made coffee, I looked at her paintings. The colors were soft and muted. Circular images swarmed randomly over the canvases. She explained to me that she approaches each piece wondering what it will reveal to her about the world, life and emotions. She seeks to learn from her paintings and to share that with those who see her works. She talked of the truth of all things being made of the circular form—atoms and cells. She talked of people needing encouragement and a listening ear more than a lecture and criticism. I was there to interview her, but she asked more questions of me. The stress of the week seemed to evaporate in her presence. When I left her studio, she gave me a beautiful painting. She said it was a favorite and that she believed I would take care of it because I understood it.

I left her home with a full stomach, a soft smile, and a wonderful memory. I also left with a new friendship. Her words were kind, generous, and truthful. Rosa does not go to church nor believe there is a single God for all people. She doesn't embrace formal religious practices, but she never lives a day without seeking to do good. She lives each day looking for an opportunity to extend grace and kindness. She believes nothing is a coincidence and all things are connected. That is spirituality. Through kind words, a warm meal, and a pause in the day, she showed me true spirituality.

Lara Smith

Sample Student Journal Exercise

TOPIC: *Describe your personal rebellion.*

Some people dye their hair green, while others pierce unusual parts of their anatomy. I, on the other hand, took a more subtle approach.

My rebellion started in kindergarten when I was forced to attend school. Why did I have to leave my cozy home to spend an entire day in a cold, unfeeling building? So I devised plans to get sent home. I knew that could cause a disturbance and get suspended, but that was not my style. Therefore, I faked a stomachache, then a sore throat, and finally the twenty-four hour flu. Over the next couple of months, I became good friends with the clinic lady. She probably saw me at least once a day, until my teacher realized what I was doing. When she stopped sending me to the clinic, I thought my rebellious days were over for good. Then came the next school year, and it started all over again.

My plan got put on the back burner because my friend, the clinic lady, was replaced. Devastatingly, a mean lady became the new clinic lady. She scared most of the kids. Once, when I was in the third grade and truly sick, I had to go to the clinic to take medicine every day for about two weeks. The clinic lady was so mean to me that I skipped a few visits, a behavior that was not at all typical for me. So I went to class every day that year, because the clinic lady would not send me home from school on the theory that I was slightly sick.

When fifth grade started, we had a new clinic lady. The mean clinic lady was replaced, and the new one was almost as nice as the first one. She and I became close friends over a short period of time. Unlike the other clinic ladies, this one did not let me get away with a lot. For some reason, though, I still liked her. The new clinic lady was strict about sending people home, but I managed one final escape. It all took place after getting my ears pierced. One of my ears became infected. It was not a big deal, and it did not even hurt. Yet, it was something that I could say hurt. My teacher eventually became annoyed with my complaining, so she sent me to the clinic.

How easy was that escape? A simple infection helped me cut class. As I grew up, I began to realize the importance of school and the foolishness of my rebellious ways. So I decided to stick with school, and I even became a pretty good student. Eventually, I even enjoyed school. My rebellious days have begun to fade away. Now I want to finish college and become a teacher. Maybe I can make school fun for the kids like me who are just looking for an excuse to go home.

Amanda Alligood

Sample Student Journal Exercise

TOPIC: *Describe your personal rebellion.*

My favorite form of personal rebellion is quite visible. I enjoy getting tattoos. I have quite a few, nine to be exact. To me, tattoos are a form of personal expression. Unfortunately, tattoos are not widely accepted in society. Aside from the personal aspect of my tattoos, I also like the culture associated with the art form, again, a culture that is widely criticized and unaccepted in general.

I think it all started when I was eighteen. I began to hang out with a friend who owned a tattoo shop, and he gave me my first tattoo. Originally, I did it to be a rebel and act out against authority, specifically, my parents. I had never done anything rebellious or against their wishes up to that point. My first one was on my upper arm. When I got it done, I was scared of what they would say, but at the same time I didn't care. I paid for it, suffered the pain, and put it on my body. Nobody could take away that tattoo or the experience away from me.

After my first tattoo, I continued to spend time at my friend's shop. I watched him do a lot of tattoos and piercing. I talked to people about tattoos I read about them as well. I began to see a culture that people who get tattoos share. I saw a culture of art, expression, and in some cases pain. I saw people get the names of family or friends who had died tattooed on their bodies. I saw faces of children, symbols, and words to remind the people getting tattooed what they were proud of and the things they had done. No matter what these people got tattooed on them or the reasons behind the tattoo, they were still going to be unaccepted by society.

Then I decided to get another tattoo. For my second tattoo, I spent more time looking at things I liked. I thought about what I wanted and what meant something to me. My second tattoo was not about rebelling against my parents as much as my first one. I wanted a piece of art. I ended up getting a fairly large tattoo on my back. The second tattoo hurt. During the tattoo, I was in pain but kept telling myself that I could get through the agony. Finally, my friend finished and handed me a mirror. As I saw the tattoo for the first time on my skin, I had the same feeling as before. "This is mine,"

I thought. I sat through the pain. Now, I have a piece of art I am pleased with.

I enjoy getting tattoos and do not see myself stopping anytime soon. Even though tattoos automatically push one towards being an outcast in society, I will not let it deter me from getting more tattoos. Tattoos express something about the people who have them, though the owner may be the only may be the only one who knows what it means to him or her. To me, tattoos represent art, freedom, and help to celebrate an individual's differences, beliefs, and experiences. Tattoos began as my rebellion, and now they are my expression.

Aaron Godbey

Additional Prompts or Heuristics for Writing about the Present

- Why do you think college is important?
- What's the difference between a "freedom fighter" and a terrorist?
- Is peace possible?
- What advice would you give a younger friend preparing for college?
- Does every question have a correct answer?
- What is in your book bag?
- What perplexes you about the opposite sex?
- What civic organizations do you belong to and how does your participation make a difference in the world?

Journal Exercise

DATE: _____

TOPIC: _____

_____

_____

_____

_____

_____

_____

_____

_____

_____

_____

_____

_____

_____

_____

_____

_____

_____

_____

_____

_____

_____

Journal Exercise

DATE: _____

TOPIC: _____

_____
_____
_____
_____
_____
_____
_____
_____
_____
_____
_____
_____
_____
_____
_____
_____
_____
_____
_____
_____
_____
_____
_____
_____
_____
_____
_____
_____
_____

Journal Exercise

DATE: _____

TOPIC: _____

_____
_____
_____
_____
_____
_____
_____
_____
_____
_____
_____
_____
_____
_____
_____
_____
_____
_____
_____
_____
_____
_____
_____
_____
_____

Journal Exercise

DATE: _____

TOPIC: _____

_____

_____

_____

_____

_____

_____

_____

_____

_____

_____

_____

_____

_____

_____

_____

_____

_____

_____

_____

_____

_____

_____

_____

_____

_____

_____

Journal Exercise

DATE: _____

TOPIC: _____

_____

_____

_____

_____

_____

_____

_____

_____

_____

_____

_____

_____

_____

_____

_____

_____

_____

_____

_____

_____

_____

_____

_____

_____

_____

_____

Journal Exercise

DATE: _____

TOPIC: _____

_____

_____

_____

_____

_____

_____

_____

_____

_____

_____

_____

_____

_____

_____

_____

_____

_____

_____

_____

_____

_____

_____

_____

_____

_____

_____

_____

_____

Journal Exercise

DATE: _____

TOPIC: _____

_____

_____

_____

_____

_____

_____

_____

_____

_____

_____

_____

_____

_____

_____

_____

_____

_____

_____

_____

_____

_____

_____

_____

_____

_____

Journal Exercise

DATE: _____

TOPIC: _____

_____

_____

_____

_____

_____

_____

_____

_____

_____

_____

_____

_____

_____

_____

_____

_____

_____

_____

_____

_____

_____

_____

_____

_____

_____

_____

_____

_____

Journal Exercise

DATE: _____

TOPIC: _____

_____
_____
_____
_____
_____
_____
_____
_____
_____
_____
_____
_____
_____
_____
_____
_____
_____
_____
_____
_____
_____
_____
_____
_____
_____
_____

Journal Exercise

DATE: _____

TOPIC: _____

_____
_____
_____
_____
_____
_____
_____
_____
_____
_____
_____
_____
_____
_____
_____
_____
_____
_____
_____
_____
_____
_____
_____
_____
_____
_____

Journal Exercise

DATE: _____

TOPIC: _____

_____
_____
_____
_____
_____
_____
_____
_____
_____
_____
_____
_____
_____
_____
_____
_____
_____
_____
_____
_____
_____
_____
_____
_____

Journal Exercise

DATE: _____

TOPIC: _____

_____

_____

_____

_____

_____

_____

_____

_____

_____

_____

_____

_____

_____

_____

_____

_____

_____

_____

_____

_____

_____

_____

_____

_____

_____

_____

_____

_____

_____

Journal Exercise

DATE: _____

TOPIC: _____

_____
_____
_____
_____
_____
_____
_____
_____
_____
_____
_____
_____
_____
_____
_____
_____
_____
_____
_____
_____
_____
_____
_____
_____
_____

Journal Exercise

DATE: _____

TOPIC: _____

_____

_____

_____

_____

_____

_____

_____

_____

_____

_____

_____

_____

_____

_____

_____

_____

_____

_____

_____

_____

_____

_____

_____

_____

_____

Journal Exercise

DATE: _____

TOPIC: _____

_____
_____
_____
_____
_____
_____
_____
_____
_____
_____
_____
_____
_____
_____
_____
_____
_____
_____
_____
_____
_____
_____
_____
_____
_____
_____

Journal Exercise

DATE: _____

TOPIC: _____

_____

_____

_____

_____

_____

_____

_____

_____

_____

_____

_____

_____

_____

_____

_____

_____

_____

_____

_____

_____

_____

_____

_____

_____

Journal Exercise

DATE: _____

TOPIC: _____

_____
_____
_____
_____
_____
_____
_____
_____
_____
_____
_____
_____
_____
_____
_____
_____
_____
_____
_____
_____
_____
_____
_____

Journal Exercise

DATE: _____

TOPIC: _____

_____

_____

_____

_____

_____

_____

_____

_____

_____

_____

_____

_____

_____

_____

_____

_____

_____

_____

_____

_____

_____

_____

_____

_____

_____

_____

_____

Journal Exercise

DATE: _____

TOPIC: _____

_____

_____

_____

_____

_____

_____

_____

_____

_____

_____

_____

_____

_____

_____

_____

_____

_____

_____

_____

_____

_____

_____

_____

_____

_____

_____

_____

Journal Exercise

DATE: _____

TOPIC: _____

_____

_____

_____

_____

_____

_____

_____

_____

_____

_____

_____

_____

_____

_____

_____

_____

_____

_____

_____

_____

_____

_____

_____

_____

_____

_____

Journal Exercise

DATE: _____

TOPIC: _____

_____
_____
_____
_____
_____
_____
_____
_____
_____
_____
_____
_____
_____
_____
_____
_____
_____
_____
_____
_____
_____
_____
_____
_____
_____
_____

Journal Exercise

DATE: _____

TOPIC: _____

_____

_____

_____

_____

_____

_____

_____

_____

_____

_____

_____

_____

_____

_____

_____

_____

_____

_____

_____

_____

_____

_____

_____

_____

Journal Exercise

DATE: _____

TOPIC: _____

_____
_____
_____
_____
_____
_____
_____
_____
_____
_____
_____
_____
_____
_____
_____
_____
_____
_____
_____
_____
_____
_____
_____
_____
_____

Journal Exercise

DATE: _____

TOPIC: _____

_____
_____
_____
_____
_____
_____
_____
_____
_____
_____
_____
_____
_____
_____
_____
_____
_____
_____
_____
_____
_____
_____
_____
_____
_____
_____
_____

Journal Exercise

DATE: _____

TOPIC: _____

_____

_____

_____

_____

_____

_____

_____

_____

_____

_____

_____

_____

_____

_____

_____

_____

_____

_____

_____

_____

_____

_____

_____

_____

Journal Exercise

DATE: _____

TOPIC: _____

_____

_____

_____

_____

_____

_____

_____

_____

_____

_____

_____

_____

_____

_____

_____

_____

_____

_____

_____

_____

_____

_____

_____

_____

_____

_____

_____

_____

Journal Exercise

DATE: _____

TOPIC: _____

_____

_____

_____

_____

_____

_____

_____

_____

_____

_____

_____

_____

_____

_____

_____

_____

_____

_____

_____

_____

_____

_____

_____

_____

_____

Journal Exercise

DATE: _____

TOPIC: _____

_____

_____

_____

_____

_____

_____

_____

_____

_____

_____

_____

_____

_____

_____

_____

_____

_____

_____

_____

_____

_____

_____

Journal Exercise

DATE: _____

TOPIC: _____

_____

_____

_____

_____

_____

_____

_____

_____

_____

_____

_____

_____

_____

_____

_____

_____

_____

_____

_____

_____

_____

_____

_____

_____

_____

_____

_____

Journal Exercise

DATE: _____

TOPIC: _____

_____
_____
_____
_____
_____
_____
_____
_____
_____
_____
_____
_____
_____
_____
_____
_____
_____
_____
_____
_____
_____
_____
_____
_____

My Voice:
Future/Deliberative

When we write about the future, we often debate what actions we should take, whether buying a car, picking a major, or casting a vote. For Aristotle, deliberative rhetoric (set in the future) usually addressed the best course of action to be taken by the state in order to ensure the happiness of the citizens. A deliberative orator or writer had to weigh evidence for and against a proposed policy, understand current law, and be in tune with local citizens' desires and fears.

For us, writing about the future offers opportunities to examine the many sides of current issues, work out our ideas about proposed legislation, analyze the best use of available resources, and understand the ramifications of controversial legal decisions.

This section provides three writing prompts and samples of student writing addressing the following topics.

• *Should foreign language classes be required?*
• *What law would you like to see repealed?*
• *Can non-violent protest work?*

The student responses are divergent and hopefully will spark your imagination. You can find additional ideas or heuristic strategies at the end of this section to help you get started writing about the present.

Sample Student Journal Exercise

TOPIC: *Should foreign language classes be required?*

Language classes and reading exams should be a requirement in higher learning as long as the student in question hasn't already had sufficient language instruction. If a person comes into college already fluent in a language in addition to English, I see no reason to force that student to learn a third one just to jump through an academic hoop.

On the other hand, in an increasingly global world and economy, the same world in which the two semester high school requirement frequently results in a student being able to count to one-hundred and to say "hello" and "how are you" and "goodbye" in another language, I think a second language is an important aspect of a well-rounded education. Not only that, I think the requirement to be able to apply that language in some provable way should be part of the requirement. Students could go into local communities and trade skills in teaching English to newcomers for a chance to practice their newly acquired language skills. Or they could be encouraged to take part in summer abroad immersion programs with cultural outcomes. Students could also participate in business internships in neighborhoods in which both English and the language they are studying is spoken.

Many Americans have argued that the world comes to us for help, wealth, and new opportunity—let that world speak our language in the asking. Yet our standard American English is not the only language of business, of science, of learning, or of community. If the student has not already stepped into a second world of language, let the journey begin in college!

Fran Holt-Underwood

Sample Student Journal Exercise

TOPIC: *Should foreign language classes be required?*

    In high school, you are required to take at least two years of a foreign language. I decided to take French instead of Spanish because I liked the way it sounded. My mom disagreed with my decision because she felt that I would never have to use French, unless I went to France, and Spanish would be more useful for my future. Well, I took two years of French and if someone asked me to say something I would only be able to recite a couple of sentences. I didn't learn very much after only two years and feel that it was a real waste of my time.

    I work in a Mexican restaurant and I have found that knowing Spanish would benefit me a lot more than knowing French. However, I don't think that foreign language should be a requirement, because it takes a very long time to become fluent in any language. Two or even four years isn't enough to really learn and be able to speak a new language well, and it really would be a waste of time if you have no need for a second language.

    Elisabeth Sherwin

Sample Student Journal Exercise

TOPIC: *What law would you like to see repealed?*

As I pass a slow-moving car on the interstate, I glare out the window with impatience on my face. I hate slow drivers or those that only go as fast as the speed limit. I cannot understand why people drive so slowly. I hate Sunday drivers. As a matter of fact, if I could repeal one law today, I would repeal the highway speed limit law. And if someone cannot handle the speed, they should stay off the road.

Not only do slow-moving vehicles get in my way, they cause more accidents than fast-moving ones do. Whenever I see cars entering the highway at a slow pace, I want to yell, "Hey, hurry up or get run over!" I hate slow drivers. Whenever cars are in the passing lane moving slowly, I just want to blow my horn to make them move. It seems like they have nothing to do but get in my way. I am so impatient. I am in such a hurry. I just need to get to wherever I need to go! I just need for Sunday drivers to get out of my way. If they would just repeal this one law, it would make my day.

Tish Nwoye

Sample Student Journal Exercise

TOPIC: *What law would you like to see repealed?*

I have always thought that city curfew laws were among the most ridiculous of legislations. The premise that mere darkness indicates the opportunity for bad things to happen seems ludicrous. Making kids be home by a certain time is not the duty of the law. In high school, my city had a curfew that stated that everyone under the age of eighteen must be off the road between the hours of one and five in the morning. While many might agree that kids have no business being out partying at that time of night, a blanket law like this assumes that all high school students live the same kind of lives and makes no contingency for emergency situations. It's definitely the role of parents to decide how late their kids can be out at night, based on their individual situations.

Another reason city curfews are stupid is because they don't work! One stipulation that our city's law had was that if a student was coming from any kind of school or work-related activity, they could not be penalized. So, of course, whenever anyone was pulled over, they just said they were coming from a football game or their job. Because anyone could come up with a perfectly good alibi so easily, the law wasn't effective at all. Also, everyone knew the chances of getting pulled over if you weren't speeding or driving recklessly were slim. I had school-sponsored play practice all the time until really late, then my friends and I would go out afterwards, sometimes for hours. Our parents knew where we were so we never worried about getting in trouble. When the concept of a law is ridiculous and it doesn't even work, something should be done differently.

Lindsey Ryan Nelms

Sample Student Journal Exercise

TOPIC: *Can non-violent protest work?*

Is non-violent protest effective? Malcolm X didn't seem to think so. But I expect that the answer to this question is contingent upon the way that the outcomes of non-violent protest are examined and surveyed. The Montgomery Bus Boycott was effective in integrating city buses, and this began with a woman who didn't even know she was protesting. Rosa Parks claimed that her famous act of defiance was merely a consequence of her being too tired from working all day to get up onto her feet and move to the back of the bus. It can even be argued that Parks' single act of non-violent protest, followed by the non-violent boycott that lasted over a year, was the vanguard of the Black Civil Rights Movement.

The rules are different, yes, but recently, a friend of mine told a story illustrating that nothing has really changed. She spoke of an upper-class condominium complex near her house. My friend drives past this gated complex on her way home from school every day and sees, sitting at the bus stop in front of the community, the black women who, she says, have obviously come from cleaning the homes and caring for the children of the people who live their. The women are waiting to step onto an integrated bus, thanks, in large part, to Rosa Parks and the citizens who participated in the Montgomery Bus Boycott, but the scene is otherwise not much different than if the year were still 1956.

If, as in the example of the boycott, non-violent protest is used to whittle away at unjust social services, then it can be effective. However, the jury is still out on whether or not non-violent protest works when the gargantuan task of restructuring dominant social, economic, and political paradigms is at hand.

Stacey Singer

Sample Student Journal Exercise

TOPIC: *Can non-violent protest work?*

Some civil rights activists have already proven that non-violent rebellion can be effective. There are many ways to get what you want without hurting other people or damaging property. Dr. Martin Luther King, Jr. showed that leading marches and many other non-violent rebellions could change the world as we know it.

Violence is abundant in the world. Even very young pre-school and elementary school students are being sent home and taken to the principal's office because of violent out lashes. If kids are learning these things in school at such a young age, how are these kids going to act when they become teenagers or adults? Their actions are only going to escalate unless they learn a lesson about how to deal with issues without violence. Talking problems out may sound a little idealistic but when it's possible, it's is the best way to solve a situation.

You can get a lot more accomplished by discussing a solution rather than punching somebody in the face and expecting conflict to suddenly stop. By acting violently nothing is accomplished to resolve the problem, the problem is just prolonged until the next encounter. Kids need to be taught at a young age that violence is wrong not by just their parents but by school counselors and other adults that have a strong influence on them.

Jamie Knack

Additional Prompts for Writing about the Future

- Should America have laws against frivolous litigation?
- Should the United States reinstate the draft?
- Should students be allowed to bring cell phones to class?
- How can America avoid dependence on foreign oil?
- How should we punish illegal music downloading?
- What should be the United States' stand on the separation of church and state?
- What books do you want to read and why?
- Should all composition courses be taught in computer classrooms?
- What are the ethical issues surrounding embryonic stem cell research?
- What will you leave at your parents' house?

Journal Exercise

DATE: _____

TOPIC: _____

_____

_____

_____

_____

_____

_____

_____

_____

_____

_____

_____

_____

_____

_____

_____

_____

_____

_____

_____

_____

_____

_____

_____

_____

Journal Exercise

DATE: _____

TOPIC: _____

_____

_____

_____

_____

_____

_____

_____

_____

_____

_____

_____

_____

_____

_____

_____

_____

_____

_____

_____

_____

_____

_____

_____

_____

_____

_____

_____

_____

_____

Journal Exercise

DATE: _____

TOPIC: _____

_____
_____
_____
_____
_____
_____
_____
_____
_____
_____
_____
_____
_____
_____
_____
_____
_____
_____
_____
_____
_____
_____
_____
_____
_____

Journal Exercise

DATE: _____

TOPIC: _____

_____

_____

_____

_____

_____

_____

_____

_____

_____

_____

_____

_____

_____

_____

_____

_____

_____

_____

_____

_____

_____

_____

_____

_____

_____

_____

Journal Exercise

DATE: _____

TOPIC: _____

_____

_____

_____

_____

_____

_____

_____

_____

_____

_____

_____

_____

_____

_____

_____

_____

_____

_____

_____

_____

_____

_____

_____

_____

_____

_____

Journal Exercise

DATE: _____

TOPIC: _____

_____

_____

_____

_____

_____

_____

_____

_____

_____

_____

_____

_____

_____

_____

_____

_____

_____

_____

_____

_____

_____

_____

_____

_____

_____

Journal Exercise

DATE: _____

TOPIC: _____

_____

_____

_____

_____

_____

_____

_____

_____

_____

_____

_____

_____

_____

_____

_____

_____

_____

_____

_____

_____

_____

_____

_____

_____

Journal Exercise

DATE: _____

TOPIC: _____

_____

_____

_____

_____

_____

_____

_____

_____

_____

_____

_____

_____

_____

_____

_____

_____

_____

_____

_____

_____

_____

_____

_____

_____

_____

Journal Exercise

DATE: _____

TOPIC: _____

_____

_____

_____

_____

_____

_____

_____

_____

_____

_____

_____

_____

_____

_____

_____

_____

_____

_____

_____

_____

_____

_____

_____

_____

_____

_____

Journal Exercise

DATE: _____

TOPIC: _____

_____
_____
_____
_____
_____
_____
_____
_____
_____
_____
_____
_____
_____
_____
_____
_____
_____
_____
_____
_____
_____
_____
_____
_____
_____

Journal Exercise

DATE: _____

TOPIC: _____

_____

_____

_____

_____

_____

_____

_____

_____

_____

_____

_____

_____

_____

_____

_____

_____

_____

_____

_____

_____

_____

_____

Journal Exercise

DATE: _____

TOPIC: _____

_____
_____
_____
_____
_____
_____
_____
_____
_____
_____
_____
_____
_____
_____
_____
_____
_____
_____
_____
_____
_____
_____
_____
_____
_____
_____
_____

Journal Exercise

DATE: _____

TOPIC: _____

_____

_____

_____

_____

_____

_____

_____

_____

_____

_____

_____

_____

_____

_____

_____

_____

_____

_____

_____

_____

_____

_____

_____

_____

_____

_____

Journal Exercise

DATE: _____

TOPIC: _____

_____

_____

_____

_____

_____

_____

_____

_____

_____

_____

_____

_____

_____

_____

_____

_____

_____

_____

_____

_____

_____

_____

_____

_____

_____

_____

_____

_____

Journal Exercise

DATE: _____

TOPIC: _____

_____
_____
_____
_____
_____
_____
_____
_____
_____
_____
_____
_____
_____
_____
_____
_____
_____
_____
_____
_____
_____
_____
_____
_____
_____
_____
_____
_____

Journal Exercise

DATE: _____

TOPIC: _____

_____

_____

_____

_____

_____

_____

_____

_____

_____

_____

_____

_____

_____

_____

_____

_____

_____

_____

_____

_____

_____

_____

_____

_____

_____

_____

Journal Exercise

DATE: _____

TOPIC: _____

_____

_____

_____

_____

_____

_____

_____

_____

_____

_____

_____

_____

_____

_____

_____

_____

_____

_____

_____

_____

_____

_____

Journal Exercise

DATE: _____

TOPIC: _____

_____

_____

_____

_____

_____

_____

_____

_____

_____

_____

_____

_____

_____

_____

_____

_____

_____

_____

_____

_____

_____

_____

_____

_____

_____

_____

Journal Exercise

DATE: _____

TOPIC: _____

_____
_____
_____
_____
_____
_____
_____
_____
_____
_____
_____
_____
_____
_____
_____
_____
_____
_____
_____
_____
_____
_____
_____
_____
_____
_____

Journal Exercise

DATE: _____

TOPIC: _____

_____

_____

_____

_____

_____

_____

_____

_____

_____

_____

_____

_____

_____

_____

_____

_____

_____

_____

_____

_____

_____

_____

_____

_____

_____

_____

_____

_____

_____

Journal Exercise

DATE: _____

TOPIC: _____

_____

_____

_____

_____

_____

_____

_____

_____

_____

_____

_____

_____

_____

_____

_____

_____

_____

_____

_____

_____

_____

_____

_____

_____

Journal Exercise

DATE: _____

TOPIC: _____

_____

_____

_____

_____

_____

_____

_____

_____

_____

_____

_____

_____

_____

_____

_____

_____

_____

_____

_____

_____

_____

_____

_____

_____

_____

_____

_____

Journal Exercise

DATE: _____

TOPIC: _____

_____

_____

_____

_____

_____

_____

_____

_____

_____

_____

_____

_____

_____

_____

_____

_____

_____

_____

_____

_____

_____

_____

_____

_____

Journal Exercise

DATE: _____

TOPIC: _____

_____
_____
_____
_____
_____
_____
_____
_____
_____
_____
_____
_____
_____
_____
_____
_____
_____
_____
_____
_____
_____
_____
_____
_____
_____
_____
_____
_____
_____
_____

Journal Exercise

DATE: _____

TOPIC: _____

_____

_____

_____

_____

_____

_____

_____

_____

_____

_____

_____

_____

_____

_____

_____

_____

_____

_____

_____

_____

_____

_____

_____

Journal Exercise

DATE: _____

TOPIC: _____

_____

_____

_____

_____

_____

_____

_____

_____

_____

_____

_____

_____

_____

_____

_____

_____

_____

_____

_____

_____

_____

_____

_____

_____

_____

_____

_____

_____

_____

Journal Exercise

DATE: _____

TOPIC: _____

_____

_____

_____

_____

_____

_____

_____

_____

_____

_____

_____

_____

_____

_____

_____

_____

_____

_____

_____

_____

_____

_____

_____

_____

_____

Journal Exercise

DATE: _____

TOPIC: _____

_____
_____
_____
_____
_____
_____
_____
_____
_____
_____
_____
_____
_____
_____
_____
_____
_____
_____
_____
_____
_____
_____
_____
_____
_____
_____

Journal Exercise

DATE: _____

TOPIC: _____

_____

_____

_____

_____

_____

_____

_____

_____

_____

_____

_____

_____

_____

_____

_____

_____

_____

_____

_____

_____

_____

_____

_____

_____

Journal Exercise

DATE: _____

TOPIC: _____

_____
_____
_____
_____
_____
_____
_____
_____
_____
_____
_____
_____
_____
_____
_____
_____
_____
_____
_____
_____
_____
_____
_____
_____
_____
_____
_____

Appendix

Heuristics and Prompts for Modes

Description

- Describe an artifact housed at a local museum or located on your campus. What do you suppose is the cultural relevance of this object?
- Visit a popular local spot. Describe the various groups of people frequenting this space. Do the groups fit stereotypical descriptions? Pay particular attention to individuals who defy normal group dynamics.
- Observe and describe children at play. What patterns of play do you see occurring in children of different ages?
- Think of your favorite item of clothing from the past or present. Describe it in detail and speculate about what makes it special to you.
- Describe a character in a book or film that you find appealing. What about this fictional person complements your own personality? Attracts you? Intrigues you?
- Design a travel brochure for your favorite place. Lure tourists to this spot through descriptive language, visual imagery, and appeals to the senses.
- Write a letter to a future descendant (your grandchild or great-grandchild) describing yourself and your culture.
- Describe a traditional meal or holiday celebration with your family or friends.
- Summarize your favorite book or movie.
- List and describe opportunities for volunteer work in your community.

Narration

- When families get together, they often repeat stories and myths that define family dynamics. Tell one of your family's oft-told stories.
- Interview someone who currently has a job in a field you plan to enter. Write a profile of that person's job as told to you firsthand.
- Write a different ending for a factual human-interest story currently in the news.
- What events in your life have helped you define your goals? Write about a pivotal moment in your past that has helped you make decisions concerning your future.
- Write an imagined story about a couple you observed in a restaurant.
- Tell the story of a time when you changed your mind about a fundamental belief.
- Write a narrative in which you illustrate this well-known childhood expression: "I am rubber, you are glue. Whatever you say bounces off me and sticks to you."
- Write a story about a time when you did something to get noticed.
- Write a short blurb advertising a book based on your life.
- When did you first realize that gender expectations and biases might limit your possibilities, freedom, or choices?

Process Analysis

- Paying close attention to audience considerations, give directions for making chocolate chip cookies to a young child, your grandmother, and Martha Stewart.
- Write a narrative in which you describe the college application process to a younger friend. Keep in mind your friend's possible frustration with the process and fear of not getting into a "good" school.
- How do you study for a big exam?
- Analyze your own writing process. Keep notes about your process as you complete a big writing assignment.

- Ask someone to put together a small Lego project or Bionicle figure following the included manufacturer's directions. Take notes as the person assembles the project, noting speed, accuracy, and frustration with the directions.
- Analyze the performance of one of your college instructors. What could this teacher do to help you learn the material better?
- Describe either a personal ritual or one you share with your friends or family. What are the steps involved in this ritual? Explain the purpose or function of the ritual.
- Write an essay in which you outline ways to get along with your enemies.
- What naturalization requirements must an immigrant pass to become a U.S. citizen?
- What criteria do you use to evaluate Web sites and online information?

Exemplification

- How is the twenty-first-century nuclear family depicted on television? Cite specific television families in your answer.
- What is the greatest act of rebellion you have witnessed?
- Choose a group that represents your values and interests. Explain the appeal of the group's core values to a non-member.
- Pick a web site that you find visually appealing. Through thick description, analyze the site's appeal to the intended audience, and use of graphics and layout.
- It's been said that everyone experiences "fifteen minutes of fame" in a lifetime. Explain this saying by recounting a time from your own life when you were famous in your community.
- Illustrate the saying "travel broadens our horizons" with examples from your own travels or experiences with other cultures.
- How does increased access to technology support the claim that "the world is getting smaller"?
- What evidence does President George W. Bush offer in support of his war on terrorism?

- Is the Internet making library research obsolete? Support your answer with concrete examples and details.
- Do women and men write differently? Explain your answer.

Cause and Effect

- Select a song that has elicited controversy in the media. After examining several opinion/editorial pieces printed against the song or performer, analyze the causes of the controversy.
- How has major industry, congestion, or local practice affected the environment in your geographical area?
- Analyze the effects of America's dependence on foreign oil.
- What do you think might be some possible legal ramifications of the Terri Schiavo case?
- Do you think parents should stay together "for the sake of the children" rather than divorce?
- Think of a time when you took a stand and didn't follow the crowd or make a popular decision. Narrate the events leading up to your decision and the consequences of going your own way.
- What are the effects of grade inflation?
- Write a letter to someone you have neglected or ignored.
- Do you have a mentor? How has that person affected your life, attitudes, ambitions, and decisions?
- How have celebrities and public figures such as Christopher Reeve, Nancy Reagan, and Michael J. Fox furthered the cause of stem cell research?

Definition

- Write a stipulative definition for a term with heavy connotations: Republican, Democrat, rebel, conservative, geek, nerd, racist, feminist.
- Define the principles by which you try to live.
- Explain your religion to someone who is unfamiliar with your belief system.

- Define courage.
- Compile a glossary of useful terms for someone new to your favorite sport or hobby.
- Define good manners for someone from a different culture.
- Define "privacy in the workplace" as it applies to regulating and monitoring Internet use.
- Do you believe your vote counts?
- What are the responsibilities and rights associated with citizenship?
- We hear politicians often talk about family values. What is your perception of family values and how have social factors influenced and shaped your opinions?

Comparison/Contrast

- Describe a place you know very well from memory. If possible, visit that place and then note discrepancies between your memories and reality.
- Establish criteria for comparing/contrasting two products you are considering purchasing: cars, stereos, a pet, etc.
- Compare/contrast two or more works by the same author, musician, or artist. Do you see a progression of ideas, a departure from familiar themes, growth as an artist?
- What do you think of cyberdating? Given the parameters of current society, online dating and matchmaking services are growing in popularity. What do you see as advantages and pitfalls of seeking a serious relationship on the Internet?
- What do you think are possible solutions to the current worries concerning social security? As life expectancy lengthens, do you think the money you are currently paying to social security will be available to you upon your retirement? Discuss possible options and alternatives to social security programs.
- Find two magazine advertisements for the same product: one from the 1970s and one current. Analyze the two ads, comparing and contrasting publishing matters, assumptions about audience, images, copy, and gender stereotypes.

- We've all heard the saying "a picture is worth a thousand words." Do you think we get a better understanding of history through photographs or written transcripts of historical events?
- Do you think teenagers and the elderly should be subjected to similar driving tests and stringent restrictions?
- What rights to education do citizens in a democracy deserve? Is higher education a right or a privilege?
- Compare and contrast morning news programs and the national nightly news. Consider the authority and attitudes of the anchors, the programs' audiences and expectations, and program content.

Classification and Division

- How do you classify yourself politically? Are you a liberal or a conservative or something in between? What influences in your life helped you form your political opinions?
- How would you categorize your family situation? Is your family typical or unique compared to the average American family ideal?
- Considering recent legislative decisions in the news, what do you think is the current status of the division of church and state in America?
- Increasing dissatisfaction with the two-party political system in the United States often leads to third-party candidates (like Ross Perot and Ralph Nader) throwing their hats into the political ring. How might the U.S. political-party system be restructured to give independent candidates (and voters) a voice and a realistic chance at election?
- What are the options for dealing with cheating, plagiarism, and academic dishonesty at your school?
- What health concerns are covered by your current health care insurance? What health issues are not addressed by your policy? What do you make of these omissions and what options exist for those in this country without comprehensive coverage?
- Reflect on the hierarchy within the U.S. military.

- Religions are often comprised of varying sects and groups. Pick a specific religion and examine the unique qualities of the various groups within that sect.
- Analyze the differences between .com, .org, .net, .gov, and .edu in web addresses.
- Categorize the various television programs you watched growing up.

Argument and Persuasion

- Explore the feasibility of publishing a magazine with your friends. Write a proposal to a potential financial backer in which you explain the various aspects associated with self-publication, including production, marketing, budget, and distribution.
- Write a restaurant review for a local newspaper. Keep in mind your audience's expectations (and perhaps limitations) concerning price, location, ambiance, variety of offerings, entertainment, etc.
- If you've been ill recently, evaluate the quality of medical care you received.
- Write a news article in which you synthesize events and speculate about possible outcomes of a current issue affecting your campus. Follow journalistic style. Include an attention-getting headline and easy-to-decipher prose. Keep in mind that people often scan newspapers and read them on the run between other activities.
- Create a visual argument (advertisement, flyer, bumper sticker, web site). What is the purpose of your argument? Who is your audience? Does your visual appeal to emotion or logic? What graphic will work best for your purposes and audience (chart, picture, cartoon, graph, famous or well-known art)?
- Analyze a print advertisement. What is the ad's "thesis"? How do the textual components, such as copy content, work with images, font, and layout? Who do you suppose is the audience for this ad? Is this advertisement effective? Explain your response.
- View a couple of episodes of a talk show based on conflict and debate (*Dr. Phil, Crossfire, Jerry Springer*). Analyze

the participants' delivery and argumentation style. What style do you find engaging and persuasive? How is the audience manipulated by the participants' persuasive tactics? Are the arguments based on fact, opinion, or emotional appeals? Which corporations sponsor the show you watched and what time of day does the program air?

- Take a stance on online courses and online degree-granting institutions. Visit the Web sites of online institutions and include an analysis of those sites in your response. Include in your argument any personal experiences with online course work or online components of traditional courses you've taken.

- Write a letter directly to the author of an essay, poem, short story, or novel that you don't like. In your letter explain why you dislike this piece. Comment on specific components of the composition that are unpleasing, offensive, or incongruent with your expectations.

- Write a dialogue between a fictional character and his or her author/creator in which the two participants discuss the development of the character.